FROM SEA to SHINING SEA

WASHINGTON, D.C.

ELINA FURMAN

Consultants

MELISSA N. MATUSEVICH, PH.D.
Curriculum and Instruction Specialist
Blacksburg, Virginia

MARGARET E. FLYNN, M.L.S.
District of Columbia Public Library
Washington, D.C.

CHILDREN'S PRESS®
A DIVISION OF SCHOLASTIC INC.

New York • Toronto • London • Auckland • Sydney • Mexico City
New Delhi • Hong Kong • Danbury, Connecticut

Washington, D.C. is located on the East Coast. It is bordered by Maryland and Virginia.

Project Editor: Meredith DeSousa
Art Director: Marie O'Neill
Photo Researcher: Marybeth Kavanagh
Design: Robin West, Ox and Company, Inc.
Page 6 map and recipe art: Susan Hunt Yule
All other maps: XNR Productions, Inc.

Library of Congress Cataloging-in-Publication Data

Furman, Elina.
     Washington, D.C. / by Elina Furman.
         p. cm.—(From sea to shining sea)
     Includes bibliographical references (p.) and index.
     Summary: Describes the geography, history, government, people, and places of
Washington, D.C.
     ISBN 0-516-22319-4
         1.Washington (D.C.) – Juvenile literature. [1. Washington (D.C.)] I. Title:
Washington, DC. II. Title. III. From sea to shining sea (Series)

F194.3 .F87 2002
975.3—dc21   2001028910

TABLE of CONTENTS

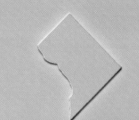

CHAPTER

ONE   Introducing the Nation's Capital **4**

TWO   The Land of Washington, D.C. **7**

THREE   Washington, D.C. Through History **15**

FOUR   Governing Washington, D.C. **41**

FIVE   The People and Places of Washington, D.C. **52**

Washington, D.C. Almanac **70**

Timeline **72**

Gallery of Famous Washingtonians **74**

Glossary **75**

For More Information **76**

Index **77**

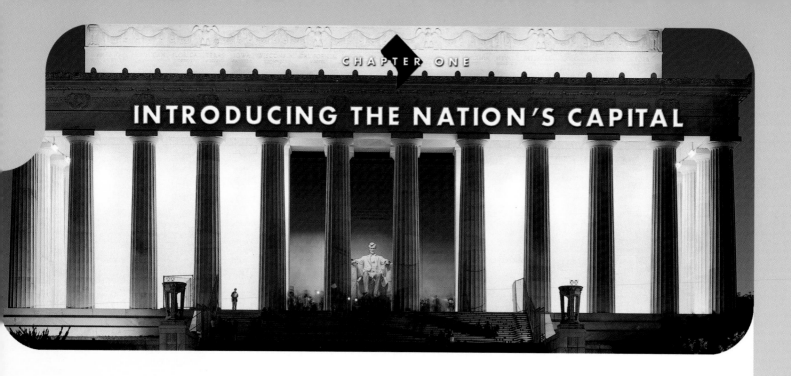

CHAPTER ONE

INTRODUCING THE NATION'S CAPITAL

Ever since it opened to the public in 1922, the Lincoln Memorial has been one of Washington, D.C.'s most popular tourist attractions.

There's something very special about Washington, D.C. What sets it apart from the rest of the country? Simply the fact that Washington, D.C. isn't a state—but a city. Unlike the states, Washington, D.C. has no representatives, senators, or governors. However, what it does have is so much more—the White House, the Capitol, the Washington Monument, the Smithsonian Institution, the Lincoln Memorial, and the honor of being our nation's capital. A country's capital is often thought to be its most important city because it is the center of its government.

Washington, D.C. is located on the East Coast, between Maryland and Virginia. With only 68 square miles (177 square kilometers) of land, it is a great deal smaller than any state in the Union. You could fit eighteen Washington, D.C.s into Rhode Island, our country's smallest state.

Washingtonians aren't concerned about the small size of their hometown. They know that although their city lacks in size and political representation, it is important to our country. To understand how important Washington, D.C. really is, consider its name. The city was named after two very important men in the history of the United States. The initials "D.C." stand for District of Columbia, named after Christopher Columbus, an early European explorer of the Americas. "Washington" is in honor of George Washington, our nation's first president. After George Washington personally chose the site of our country's capital, people began calling it "the city of Washington."

What comes to mind when you think of Washington, D.C.?

- Presidents leading the country from the White House
- Monuments in honor of famous historical figures
- Students attending Washington's many universities
- Cherry trees blossoming around the Tidal Basin
- The Capitol dome towering over the city
- People hiking and biking in Rock Creek Park
- American soldiers fighting against British soldiers during the War of 1812
- Congressmen passing laws on Capitol Hill
- Tourists enjoying the city's parks, museums, and restaurants

Our nation's capital involves many great people and has a distinguished history. Turn the page to discover how Washington, D.C. has lived up to its name.

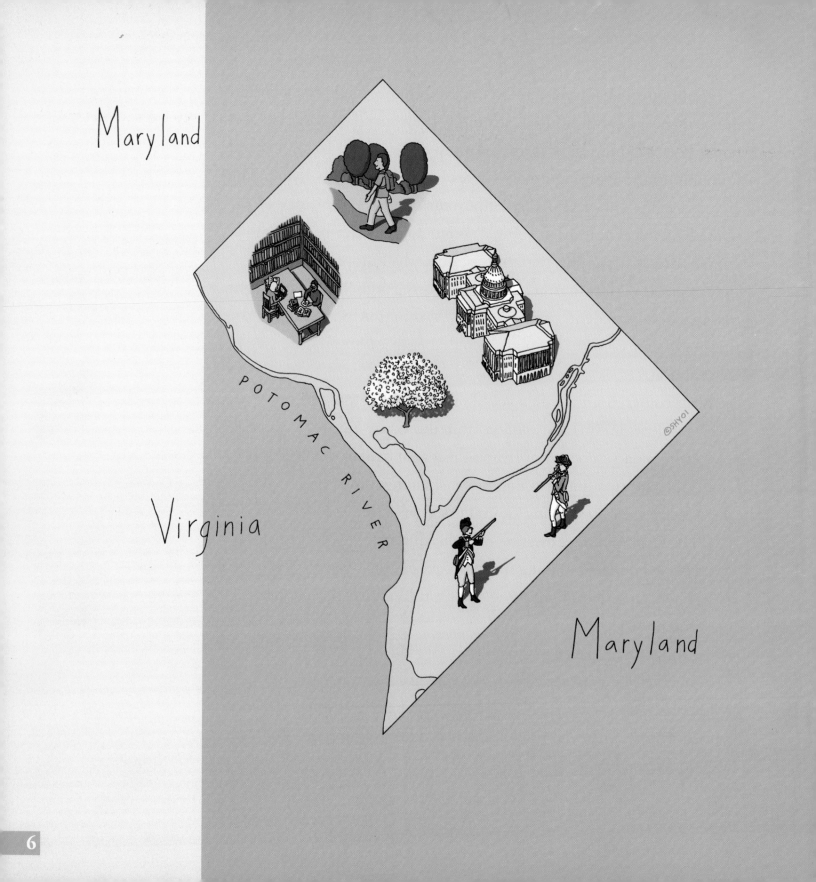

Maryland

Virginia

POTOMAC RIVER

Maryland

CHAPTER TWO

THE LAND OF WASHINGTON, D.C.

The Georgetown Rowing Crew practices on the Potomac River.

If you look at a map of the United States, you'll see that Washington, D.C. is roughly a diamond-shaped area located on the East Coast. The city is situated on the border of Maryland and Virginia. Maryland lies to the northeast, and Virginia is located to the southwest. You might also notice that Washington, D.C. is one in a long line of big cities along the Atlantic coast dotting the eastern seaboard. Starting at Boston, Massachusetts, and moving south, you'll pass through New York City, Philadelphia, and Baltimore before arriving at Washington, D.C.

On most maps, Washington, D.C. is represented by a star instead of a dot, which is the usual map symbol for a city. The star means that Washington, D.C. is our nation's capital. You'll also notice that its borders are not solid like those of its neighbors, Virginia and Maryland. Instead, they are marked by a dotted line to indicate that Washington, D.C. is not a state, but an important city.

These Washingtonians are taking time out to bicycle in Rock Creek Park.

THE LANDSCAPE

Although Washington, D.C. is very much a city, it is also blessed with much natural beauty. From cherry trees to wildflowers, the land of Washington provides a scenic backdrop for many of our nation's most important buildings.

Just five miles (8 kilometers) north of the White House is a large forest in the valley of Rock Creek. Rock Creek runs the length of the city, and Rock Creek Park offers a quiet getaway from the city bustle. It is one of the largest forested urban parks in the United States, and in 1890 it was designated a national park. Rock Creek Park's 2,820 acres (1,142 hectares) of woodland contain a rushing creek and deep gorges, as well as gently sloping hills and grassy meadows. Park trails provide opportunities for hiking, biking, skating, and horseback riding.

Washington's natural beauty is not restricted to Rock Creek Park.

The entire District of Columbia is covered in gently sloping hills. They don't call the site of the Capitol building "Capitol Hill" for nothing—at 88 feet (27 meters) above the Potomac River, it was once the highest point in Washington, D.C.

The Tidal Basin is in southwest D.C., inside the banks of the Potomac River. The edge of the Basin is lined with 3,700 cherry trees. Thousands of tourists visit every spring, when the trees sprout pretty pink and white blossoms.

RIVERS AND STREAMS

The border of Maryland and Virginia, where Washington, D.C. is located, is formed by the Potomac River. The river forms what is known as a natural boundary. The Potomac is the main river in Washington, D.C., and it gives the city much of its natural charm.

The Potomac runs southeast for 383 miles (616 kilometers) from its source in the Allegheny Mountains to its mouth in the Chesapeake Bay, southeast of Washington, D.C. The Potomac divides into two branches

Blossoming cherry trees add to the scenic landscape of Washington, D.C.

at Cumberland, Maryland. Boats and ships can sail on the Potomac, but only between the Chesapeake Bay and Washington, D.C. North of the city, the calm Potomac grows wild, turning into rapids and cascades. One of the Potomac's most spectacular attractions is Great Falls, located just a few miles from Washington, D.C.

In the Great Falls area, the Potomac River picks up speed and flows over steep, jagged rocks.

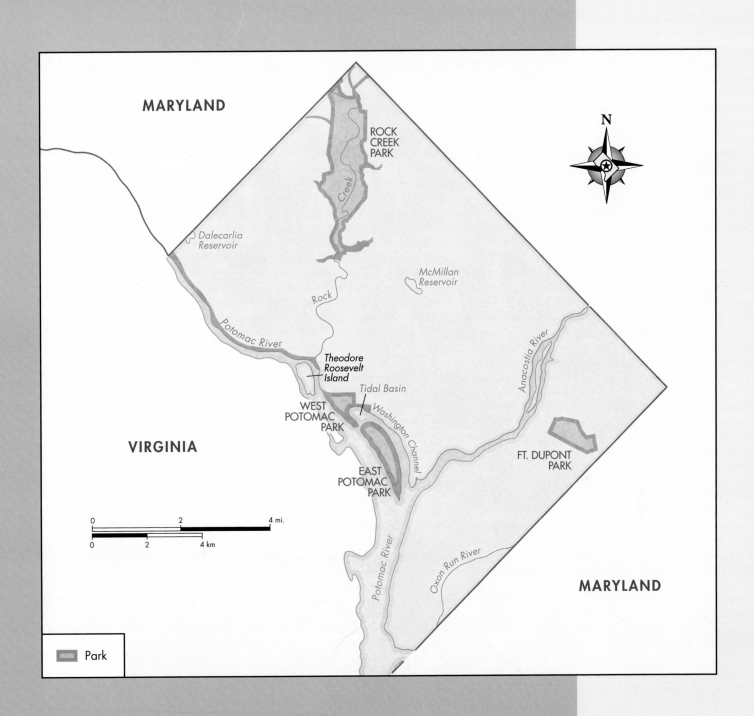

MARYLAND

ROCK
CREEK
PARK

Creek

*Dalecarlia
Reservoir*

*McMillan
Reservoir*

Rock

Potomac River

Anacostia River

*Theodore
Roosevelt
Island*

Tidal Basin

WEST
POTOMAC
PARK

Washington Channel

VIRGINIA

EAST
POTOMAC
PARK

FT. DUPONT
PARK

MARYLAND

0   2   4 mi.

0   2   4 km

Potomac River

Oxon Run River

Park

FIND OUT MORE

One reason that Washington, D.C. was built on the banks of the Potomac River is because the river had two tobacco ports. One was in Georgetown, Maryland, and the other in Alexandria, Virginia. In the early 1800s, ships would pick up and unload tobacco at these harbors. How do you think these ports helped the early settlements of Washington, D.C. to develop?

Like most large rivers, the Potomac has tributaries, or smaller rivers that flow into it. One of the Potomac's tributaries is the Anacostia River. Its source is about 20 miles (32 kilometers) northeast of Washington, D.C. in College Park, Maryland. The Anacostia flows through the southeast portion of the city before feeding into the Potomac.

Hundreds of years ago, many fish lived in the Anacostia. In 1632, a visitor wrote that "the Indians in one night commonly will catch thirty sturgeon. . . . And as for deer, buffaloes, and turkeys, the woods do swarm with them, and the soil is . . . fertile." Today, there is very little life left in the river because of overfishing and water pollution.

Washington is also home to Rock Creek. This long and winding stream flows south through Maryland and Washington, D.C. before it unites with the Potomac.

CLIMATE

Washington, D.C. enjoys four distinct seasons, but most Washingtonians will tell you that spring and fall are their favorites. Summers are usually too hot and humid for comfort. The average temperature during summer is around 77° Fahrenheit (25° Celsius), although sometimes it gets as hot as 100°F (38°C). On July 20, 1930, the temperature climbed to 106°F (41°C)—the hottest day in D.C. history.

Winters are not much better. With more rain than snow, Washington, D.C. has very cold winters. Temperatures often dip below 30°F (−1°C). On February 11, 1899, the temperature dropped to −15°F (−26°C)! A huge snowstorm followed shortly after, dumping more than 20 inches (51 centimeters) of snow. That year, the city also saw its record snowfall—54 inches (137 cm).

The capital falls calm and quiet under cover of a winter evening.

Snowstorms are not common, however, and usually catch residents unprepared. The city gets about 40 inches (102 cm) of precipitation, mostly in the form of rain, over the course of one year. August is a particularly rainy month.

Most people agree that spring is the best time of year in D.C. The rain may not stop completely, but the cherry trees bloom between late March and early April. Washington's fall season is another favorite for tourists and residents. The mild temperatures and rich colors of the city's many trees make autumn in D.C. a nature-lover's paradise.

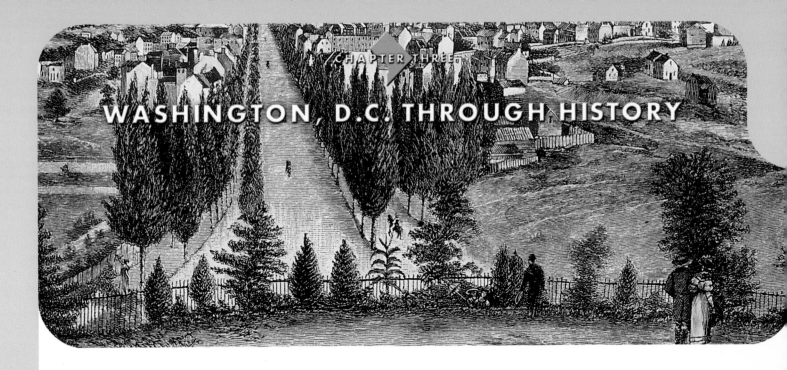

CHAPTER THREE

WASHINGTON, D.C. THROUGH HISTORY

Washington, D.C. was once covered with forests, prairies, marshes, and rivers. Before the arrival of European settlers, the Nacotchtank (or Nachotanke) Indians of the Piscataway Native American tribe were the only inhabitants of this land. For 3,000 years, the Nacotchtank lived in villages throughout the area. Their dwellings were usually located in the forests, on the prairies, and on the banks of the Potomac and Anacostia Rivers.

The Nacotchtank considered the land along the Potomac to be sacred ground. They respected the land, because growing corn and other crops in the fertile soil was very easy. They grew corn and beans, hunted deer, turkey, and buffalo, and fished in the rivers and streams. The Nacotchtank were part of the larger tribe of Piscataway Indians that was led by the great chief of Piscataway, but the smaller Nacotchtank settlement was ruled by its own chief.

This drawing shows a view of Washington, D.C. in 1800.

In 1608, English Captain John Smith was the first person to sail as far as Washington on the Potomac. With a crew of 14 men, Smith made maps of the area and recorded his visit in a journal. Upon his arrival he met Native Americans there and wrote that "the people did their best to content us." He left without attempting to start a settlement in the area.

In 1632, England's George Calvert, also known as Lord Baltimore, was given what is now Maryland by King Charles I. Lord Baltimore was a Roman Catholic. He wanted to make Maryland a safe place for other Catholics who were being persecuted in England by the Protestants, who tried to prevent them from practicing their religion.

In 1634, Lord Baltimore's son, Leonard Calvert, sailed to Maryland with 20 gentlemen, 300 workers, and two Catholic priests from England. After reaching Maryland, a fur trader named Henry Fleete accompanied Calvert further up the Potomac, into what is now Washington. They wanted to seek permission from Native Americans to start a settlement there, and Fleete could speak the language of the Piscataway Indians. When Calvert and Fleete arrived, the great chief of the Piscataway tribe was friendly but turned them away.

In the meantime, Calvert's settlers were establishing villages and farms south of Washington. There, the Europeans carried on trade with friendlier Native American tribes. Thanks to the American Indians, the colonists learned about growing and cooking corn, which became an

important part of their diet. The colonists also hunted rabbit, pigeon, and deer.

Early colonists in the Washington area fished in the Potomac River.

DECLINE OF THE PISCATAWAY

Life for the Piscataway became difficult once European settlers arrived in the area. Lord Calvert frequently tried to convert them to the

Catholic religion, despite the fact that they practiced their own religion. Also, European settlers brought contagious diseases such as measles and smallpox into the area. Most natives who caught these diseases did not know how to treat them, nor were their bodies able to fight these unfamiliar diseases. As a result, many Native Americans died.

It wasn't long before the settlers wanted more land. Another nearby tribe, the Susquehannocks, also wanted land belonging to the Piscataways. The Susquehannocks frequently attacked them, raiding their villages. The Piscataway population went from 2,500 to less than 400. By 1700, most Piscataways had been driven off their land and moved north and west.

DEVELOPING THE SITE

The colonists soon discovered they could grow tobacco and other crops on the rich soil surrounding the Potomac River. They divided the land into farms. The largest farms were called plantations, or manors. Plantations were owned by members of the aristocracy, England's wealthiest classes, because they could afford to hire laborers and buy African slaves to work in their fields.

Slavery was a common practice in the English colonies. Slaves were taken from their homes in Africa and brought to the colonies on ships. There, they were bought by settlers and forced to do backbreaking farm labor without pay. The settlers considered slaves a necessity in order to keep the plantations going, because slaves worked for free. Without hav-

Slaves were sold to plantation owners at markets or auctions.

ing to pay wages to field workers, plantation owners were able to make a large profit.

Poor, working class people who could not afford to buy slaves or hire help received much smaller farms that they worked themselves. Often, they found jobs as tenant farmers on manors, where they rented land and paid for it with a portion of their crops. This was called the manorial system. Other settlers worked as craftsmen and laborers.

Although plantations were scattered throughout the area, much of Washington, D.C. was covered with marshes and woods. Each tobacco

Much of the early Washington area was wooded and marshy.

plantation was its own, sprawling community. The only town was St. Mary's City, Maryland, near the mouth of the Potomac.

Georgetown was established near the Potomac River in 1752. The settlement was built on land bought from two men, George Gordon and George Beall. The town was named in honor of King George II of England. Georgetown soon developed into a profitable shipping community because of its ready access to the Potomac. What began as a shipping center for tobacco soon developed into a commercial hub, with mills and wharves built near the waterfront.

In 1765, an area east of Georgetown, originally called Funkstown, became a factory town. German immigrant Jacob Funk bought 130 acres (53 hectares) of land to house his factories, including a woolen mill, a paper mill, and a powder mill. Funkstown soon became the industrial center of Washington, D.C. The area eventually became known as Foggy Bottom because it used to be very swampy and often covered by a thick fog. Now the fog is mixed with smoke from the factories and has become thick smog.

WASHINGTON, D.C. IN REVOLUTIONARY TIMES

At this time, the land that is now Washington, D.C. was part of the Virginia and Maryland colonies. Like the other colonies, they were part of a larger territory that was claimed by England. Colonists paid taxes to the English government. However, unlike citizens of England, they had no voting rights in Parliament, England's main governing body.

To raise money, England imposed taxes on many goods that were sold to the colonists, such as paper and tea. Many colonists felt that the taxes were unfair because the colonies were not represented in English government. They protested by staging riots and demonstrations, and eventually some of the taxes were repealed, or taken away. New taxes were imposed, however, and the colonists became more frustrated with the English government.

On July 4, 1776, representatives from twelve English colonies adopted the Declaration of Independence. This important document stated reasons why the colonies should be independent from England, and declared their intent to form their own government. Four representatives signed the Declaration of Independence on behalf of everyone in Maryland.

Members from the Second Continental Congress gathered to sign the Declaration of Independence on August 2, 1776, almost a month after it was officially adopted.

England wasn't about to let the colonies go without a fight. This fight is most often called the War for Independence, or the American Revolution (1775–1783). British soldiers sailed across the Atlantic to recapture the colonies. During the war, some Washington, D.C. residents fought in the army. Others stayed on their plantations to oversee the harvesting of tobacco. When the war came to an end, the colonies were victorious and the United States was born. At this time, Washington, D.C. was still part of Maryland and Virginia. The United States had not yet decided on a permanent capital.

FIND OUT MORE

People have been paying taxes since ancient times. Even today, United States citizens pay taxes to the government on the money they earn. The money raised by taxes is used to provide public services for citizens. What are some of the services our taxes are used for?

Temporary capitals were set up in New York City and Philadelphia. The members of the newly formed United States Congress, a group of people selected to create the country's laws, moved from city to city in order to hold meetings. In 1777, Congress met in Baltimore, Philadelphia, New York, and Lancaster.

This arrangement created problems. People traveled by horse and carriage, and after ten years of moving around in this fashion, lawmakers grew weary. Everyone agreed that the new United States government needed a permanent home. The only question was where? The northern states wanted the capital in the North, and the southern states wanted it in the South.

In 1787, eleven years after signing the Declaration of Independence, Congress drafted another document called the United States Constitution. The Constitution explained the structure of the new government and its laws. In 1789, Congress elected George Washington the first president and John Adams vice president. But Congress was still no closer to solving the problem of the national capital. Representatives from North and South could not agree. The friction between the two sides was at an all-time high.

Finally, on July 10, 1790, North and South arrived at a compromise. The South could have the capital if the federal government

WHO'S WHO IN WASHINGTON, D.C.?

George Washington (1732–1799) was the first president of the United States. The thirteen English colonies became the United States under his leadership. He served as commander in chief during the American Revolution, and took a leading role in the creation of the Constitution. Washington was born in Westmoreland County, Virginia, and later lived in Mount Vernon, Virginia.

agreed to pay off the Northern states' large Revolutionary War debts. It was decided that the capital, called Federal City, would be built along the Potomac River on land that belonged to Maryland and Virginia. This was the first time in history—and in the world—that a city was to be built for the specific purpose of becoming a national capital. The Federal City was under construction for ten years. During this time, from 1790 until 1800, Philadelphia served as the temporary capital.

BUILDING THE CAPITAL

Once the general location was decided upon, George Washington chose the one hundred-square-mile (259-sq-km) site that would become Washington, D.C. Many people believe he chose the site because it was close to his home in Mount Vernon, Virginia. Both Maryland and Virginia agreed to donate territory for construction of the capital city.

George Washington began planning the construction of Federal City with the help of French architect Pierre Charles L'Enfant. As the architect, L'Enfant was responsible for planning, designing, engineering, and building the city. This was a difficult undertaking. The area was rural and undeveloped. The shores of the Potomac were wet and marshy. To make matters worse, Washington first needed to convince

The cornerstone of the Capitol was laid by President Washington on September 18, 1793.

Pierre Charles L'Enfant designed the original plan for Washington in 1791.

the landowners to sell their land to the government before the capital city could be built.

Washington was successful in convincing the landowners to sell. There was just one catch—the landlords would not receive money for land that became streets and avenues. Unaware of L'Enfant's plans for the city, the landowners agreed to the deal. Imagine their surprise when they learned that L'Enfant wanted to use more than half of their land just for streets and avenues! This meant that the landowners' deal with Washington wasn't as profitable as they had hoped.

Andrew Ellicott had a good relationship with landowners and political leaders.

Still, L'Enfant carried on with his plans. He planned the White House, the Capitol building, and the entire layout of what is now Washington, D.C. His ideas were inspired, but his methods left much to be desired. He had a temperamental nature and often clashed with members of Congress. When L'Enfant tore down the home of an important landowner without permission, George Washington had no choice but to replace him.

L'Enfant's replacement was a man named Andrew Ellicott. Ellicott was assisted by Benjamin Banneker, who had worked with L'Enfant on the original plans. Although L'Enfant had taken the plans when he left, Banneker was able to reproduce them from memory, and the project continued where it had left off.

WHO'S WHO IN WASHINGTON, D.C.?

Benjamin Banneker (1731–1806) was an African-American scientist and mathematician who helped to plan the city of Washington, D.C. Also a skilled astronomer, Banneker published an annual *Farmer's Almanac* from 1792 to 1802. The almanac contained mathematical calculations showing the position of the planets. It became so popular that Banneker gained respect in places as far away as England and France. He used his reputation to effect change for the equal rights of African-Americans. Banneker was born in Maryland.

George Washington's second term as president came to an end in 1797. After retiring to his plantation in Mount Vernon, Virginia, he died on December 14, 1799. Just six months later, the seat of government was moved to Washington, D.C. once and for all. Federal City was renamed Washington, after the leader who had helped build the city. The entire surrounding area was called the District of Columbia.

THE EARLY YEARS

Washington wasn't a pretty sight in the early days. The streets were unpaved, buildings were unfinished, and farm animals roamed the avenues. But right from the start it was clear that Washington, D.C. would be an interesting place to live, despite its ramshackle appearance. City residents had a front-row seat to the nation's politics, which often proved entertaining. For example, when John Adams, the second president, lost the 1800 presidential campaign to Thomas Jefferson, he didn't attend Jefferson's inauguration, which resulted in much talk around the city.

Presidential receptions were common in the early days of Washington, D.C.

During the War of 1812, British troops set fire to the White House.

In 1802, city residents were given the right to elect their own city council. The mayor, however, was appointed by the president. It wasn't until 1820 that Congress finally granted the residents of Washington, D.C. the right to elect their own mayor.

Over time, the city began taking shape. The Capitol was almost complete by 1811, and new buildings were in progress, including a treasury and a post office. Private residences were also being built.

Everything was going according to plan until 1812, when war broke out between the United States and England. The War of 1812 (1812–1815) began when Congress declared war on England, and the British responded by sending their troops across the Atlantic. When the British landed on United States shores, they marched on Washington. In 1814, they invaded the capital city and set fire to many new buildings, including the White House. The British would surely have pressed on with their march had a strong windstorm not caught them off guard and forced them to turn back. After the war ended, it took the United States until 1819 to restore Washington, D.C.'s buildings to their former glory.

For the next forty years, the United States rapidly expanded to the west. Washington, D.C., on the other hand, grew at a very slow pace. You might even say it got smaller. In 1846, Alexandria County on the southwest bank of the Potomac was returned to Virginia. The rest of the city was making slow progress. Roads in Washington were still unpaved, cows and pigs continued to roam the streets, and there were very few people or homes within the city. Some even described Washington, D.C. as a "sea of mud." All this would change with the onset of the Civil War in 1861.

FIND OUT MORE

Washington, D.C. began with an area of 100 square miles (259 sq km). When Alexandria County was returned to the state of Virginia in 1846, Washington was left with slightly more than 68 square miles (177 sq km). How many square miles of land did Washington, D.C. lose?

THE CIVIL WAR

In 1860, Abraham Lincoln was elected president. During this time, there was growing discontent between North and South over many issues, including slavery. The mostly rural South made its money from cotton plantations and tobacco fields, which depended on slave labor. In the industrialized North, most people earned a living by doing factory work, where they were paid wages. In many parts of the North, slavery was illegal.

Abraham Lincoln was against the spread of slavery, and the South feared that he would try to abolish it, putting an end to slavery within the United States. In protest, several southern states seceded from the union and formed a new nation called the Confederate States of America. Tension between the two sides increased, and in April 1861 the Civil War (1861–1865) began. Most Northerners fought on the Union side, and many Southerners fought for the Confederacy.

Abraham Lincoln began serving as president in 1861.

During the war, Washington, D.C. was turned into a military base. Buildings such as the Capitol and the National Archives were turned into the army's sleeping quarters, cafeterias, warehouses, and hospitals. Thousands of Union troops were stationed in the city to protect it from Confederate attacks. In addition, many escaped slaves entered Washington from the South, especially after Lincoln issued the Emancipation Proclamation in 1863. The Emancipation Proclamation freed all slaves in the South under the condition of military victory for the North. As a result, many slaves joined the Union Army and Navy. Washington's

Members of the Eighth Regiment Massachusetts Volunteer Militia gathered inside the Capitol during the Civil War.

population nearly doubled during the war, jumping from about 60,000 to 120,000.

The war ended in April 1865, with the Union having triumphed over the Confederacy. Five days after the Confederate Army surrendered, Abraham Lincoln was assassinated in Washington by John Wilkes Booth, a Confederate supporter. Lincoln was killed while watching a play at Ford's Theatre. As the news of his death spread, a terrible sadness was felt by many Washingtonians, as well as by many others throughout the United States.

This drawing shows John Wilkes Booth fleeing the scene after assassinating President Lincoln at Ford's Theatre.

FAMOUS FIRSTS

- Washington, D.C. was the first city designed for the purpose of becoming a nation's capital
- Georgetown University was the nation's first Catholic college, founded in 1789
- The first official long-distance telegraphic message in Morse Code was sent from Washington, D.C. to Baltimore, Maryland, in 1844

The United States and the Emancipation Proclamation lived on. In fact, slavery was outlawed in Washington, D.C. even before the Emancipation Proclamation abolished slavery in the South. After the war, many former slaves left their plantations and found refuge in Washington, D.C. By the turn of the century, the city had the highest African-American population of any city in the country.

The constant flow of new arrivals put a strain on the city's resources. More homes, roads, churches, and schools were built. New businesses were started. The city was so crowded that some areas overflowed with poor people and run-down shacks. By 1870, there were more than 130,000 residents of Washington.

In 1874, the government of Washington, D.C. was deeply in debt. Sloppy business practices and overspending left the city bankrupt. Congress was appalled at the city's mismanagement and they took control. They decided that the District of Columbia would be managed by three commissioners appointed by the presi-

This drawing by W. Bengough shows the crowded conditions of the Old Congressional Library in the 1890s.

dent. Once again, the citizens had no voice in their city's government.

In 1871, the city of Georgetown gave up its independent charter and became part of Washington. It was at this point that Washington and the District of Columbia became unified under one charter, an official document granting rights to the new city. The city now counted nearly 140,000 residents, and the population showed no signs of slowing down.

WHAT'S IN A NAME?

Some of the names of places in and around Washington, D.C. have interesting origins.

Name	Comes From or Means
District of Columbia	Christopher Columbus, explorer who discovered the New World
Baltimore	Lord Baltimore, founder of Maryland
Georgetown	King George II of England
Anacostia	Named after the Anacostan Indian tribes

WASHINGTON, D.C. IN THE 20TH CENTURY

At the turn of the last century, the government decided to expand on L'Enfant's original plan for the city. The revised plan of 1901 was called the McMillan Model, and it was based on the design of other "great cities" in Europe, such as Vienna and Paris. From this model came the design of the National Mall, the Lincoln Memorial, and other parts of the city. Monuments and museums, as well as university and government buildings, began cropping up all over the District.

The nation's capital grew more important as the United States gained influence on world events. Our country's decision to enter World War I (1914–1918) was handed down from Washington, D.C. in 1917. The

war led to yet another period of growth. The government needed more workers to direct the war effort, and by 1920 there were more than 440,000 people in Washington. The war ended in victory for the United States and its allies, and a huge victory parade was held on Pennsylvania Avenue.

THE GREAT DEPRESSION

In 1929, hard times fell on Washington, D.C. and the rest of the United States. That year, the stock market plummeted and people around the country lost large amounts of money due to the declining value of their business investments. As a result, they spent less money buying goods, and businesses were unable to sell their products. Many businesses closed, leaving thousands of people unemployed. Banks also closed, leaving even more people penniless. One in every four people was out of work. This period is known as the Great Depression (1929–1939).

In June 1932, hungry and frustrated citizens took their troubles to Washington. More than 20,000 veterans, or soldiers, of World War I marched on Washington to request payment (a "bonus") for their service during the war. In what became known as the "Bonus March," vet-

Bonus marchers camped out in small huts to demand payment for their war service.

erans demanded that the government pay them what had been promised years before. Marchers stayed in the city for weeks, setting up camp and living in cardboard boxes. In late July, President Herbert Hoover tried to disperse the angry mob with the use of tear gas and tanks, and two bonus marchers were shot by police. Although the marchers were eventually forced out of the city, the event became an embarrassment for the president and contributed to his defeat in the next presidential election.

President Franklin D. Roosevelt helped pull the country out of the Great Depression.

In November 1933, Franklin Delano Roosevelt was elected president. To help bring the United States out of the Depression, Roosevelt started a program called the New Deal. The programs of the New Deal expanded the role of government and created many new government jobs in Washington, D.C. More people moved to the city to fill the newly created jobs.

By 1950, the city was overflowing with residents. However, the population would soon start to decline. President Dwight Eisenhower made great progress in building roads called highways that would help people travel at faster speeds between the suburbs and the cities. Construction on new housing developments began to take place in areas just outside of Washington, and many people left the city to live in the suburbs of Maryland and Virginia.

THE CIVIL RIGHTS MOVEMENT

In 1963, Washington, D.C. was the scene of an important event in the civil rights movement. During this time, African-Americans were struggling to gain equality. They held nonviolent protests and demonstrations throughout the United States in the late 1950s and early 1960s. On August 28, 1963, more than 250,000 Americans arrived in Washington, D.C. to show their support for a new civil rights bill proposed by President John F. Kennedy. Many artists and civil rights leaders, including famous leader Martin Luther King Jr., sang songs and delivered speeches. Despite the fact that the bill was not passed until nearly a year later, the day was considered an overwhelming success.

A few years later, in 1968, Martin Luther King Jr. was assassinated in Memphis, Tennessee. He had been a great leader and a symbol of hope for the African-American community, and many people—black and white—mourned his loss. Some people were so angry that they formed large crowds and began to riot. While riots went on in many cities, some of the worst riots took place in Washington, D.C. Angry mobs of people burst out onto the streets, breaking storefront windows, turning over cars, and stealing property to show their frustration. This frightening event led people to believe that Washington, D.C., was not a safe place to live. Still more people fled the city for the suburbs.

Martin Luther King Jr.'s most famous speech, "I Have a Dream," was delivered during the 1963 March on Washington.

As the center of American government, Washington, D.C. is often in the national spotlight, for better or worse. One of the most famous political scandals, now known as "Watergate," took place in Washington in 1972. Located in Foggy Bottom, Watergate is a hotel and apartment complex where many government workers live. On the night of June 17, 1972, burglars broke into the building to spy on people who worked in government offices there. It was later discovered that President Nixon was secretly involved in the break-in, and the incident ultimately led to his resignation from office.

The Watergate Hotel (now called Swissotel, The Watergate) was made famous by the burglary scandal involving Richard Nixon.

In 2001, a suburb of Washington, D.C. received a great deal of national attention. The headquarters of the United States armed forces is in the Pentagon, a building located in Arlington, Virginia, on the west bank of the Potomac River. On September 11, terrorists seized control of a commercial plane and sent it crashing into the Pentagon, leaving a hole on one side of the building and setting it on fire. At about the same time, two other planes crashed into the World Trade Center in New York City, and a fourth plane crashed into the ground in Pennsylvania. Nearly 200 people died as a result of the attack on the Pentagon.

The Pentagon, located just outside Washington, D.C., is one of the world's largest office buildings.

Although Washington, D.C. has been through difficult times, it will always be the most important city in our nation. It is a bustling metropolis filled with national treasures. Its many monuments and museums capture our nation's history, while its government buildings and national leaders symbolize the strength of our country's future.

CHAPTER FOUR

GOVERNING WASHINGTON, D.C.

The United States government is located in Washington, D.C., but where is the city's local government? Although there is no governor in Washington, it is not a lawless city. The District has a local government that handles city affairs. There are three branches, or parts, that govern the District—the executive, the legislative, and the judicial. The mayor is head of the executive branch, and a 13-member council serves as the legislative branch.

The White House still closely resembles the way it looked when it was reconstructed in 1815.

EXECUTIVE BRANCH

The executive branch enforces the city's laws. The mayor is head of the executive branch. He or she works with independent agencies to ensure that the city runs smoothly, in everything from transportation and schools to housing and communities. The mayor has the power to veto

Anthony Williams has served as Washington, D.C.'s mayor since 1999.

bills (new laws) that are proposed by the city council, and may refuse to sign them into law.

The mayor of Washington, D.C. is elected by city residents to serve a four-year term. He or she appoints four people to serve on the board of education, and selects many other people to take charge of special departments such as the energy office, the department of health, and the department of housing and community development.

LEGISLATIVE BRANCH

The legislative branch passes local laws. In Washington, D.C., an organization called the city council serves as the legislative branch. Council members pass laws relating to a variety of subjects, such as motor vehicle safety and the building of roads or schools. In addition, the council approves the budget, which determines how the city's money will be spent.

The council is made up of thirteen members. Five council members are elected by the entire city, and the other eight members are elected by parts of the city, called wards, that they will represent. Washington, D.C. has eight wards. Council members serve four-year terms. One member is named chairperson of the council and represents the entire district. The chairperson is a lot like the vice president; if the mayor is unable to finish serving his or her term, the chairperson of the legislative council will take the mayor's place.

JUDICIAL BRANCH

The judicial branch interprets the laws. This is done through the city's court system. The District of Columbia court system is made up of a court of appeals and a superior court. Many cases begin in superior court. If one of the parties is not satisfied with the court's decision they may request an appeal, or rehearing of the case, in the court of appeals. The court of appeals is the highest court in Washington, D.C., with eight associate judges and a Chief Judge serving on the court.

WASHINGTON, D.C. MAYORS

Name	Term
Walter Washington	1975–1979
Marion Barry	1979–1991
Sharon Pratt Kelly	1991–1995
Marion Barry	1995–1999
Anthony Williams	1999–

HISTORY OF CITY GOVERNMENT

The District of Columbia's government has undergone many changes since the city was first established in 1790. At that time, one of the requirements for statehood was a population of 50,000. With only 3,000 residents, Washington did not qualify. Instead of a locally elected government, the area was managed by three commissioners who were appointed by George Washington.

In 1800, Congress determined that the District's residents would be governed by the laws of Virginia and Maryland. Those who lived on the Virginia side of the Potomac would abide by Virginia laws, and those who lived on the Maryland side were subject to Maryland's laws. This arrangement didn't last long. The residents of Washington wanted to have their own government. As locals, they weren't allowed to vote for the state government of Maryland or Virginia. So why should they have to pay taxes to the states and follow their laws? Two years later, they convinced Congress to let Washington, D.C. become a city with its own council and a mayor. The residents voted for the council members, and the president appointed the mayor.

Throughout the 1800s, several changes took place in the city's government, including some that took away the residents' rights to elect their own leaders. Before 1963, the people living in the District of Columbia were the only United States citizens without the right to vote for our country's president and vice president.

Although Washington, D.C. is home to the Capitol, its residents have no representatives in Congress. This photo shows legislators gathered inside the Capitol to hear a presidential address.

WASHINGTON, D.C. GOVERNMENT

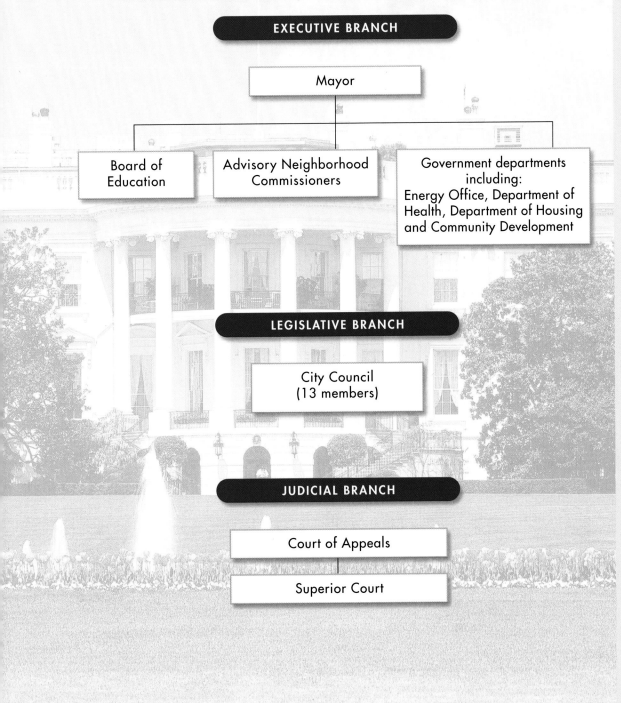

EXECUTIVE BRANCH

Mayor

Board of Education

Advisory Neighborhood Commissioners

Government departments including:
Energy Office, Department of Health, Department of Housing and Community Development

LEGISLATIVE BRANCH

City Council (13 members)

JUDICIAL BRANCH

Court of Appeals

Superior Court

In 1967, the three commissioners in charge of Washington were replaced by a presidentially-appointed mayor and city council. Six years later, Congress passed the Home Rule Act. This Act allowed the residents of Washington to elect their own mayor and city council. It's likely that we haven't seen the last of the changes in Washington, D.C.'s local government.

A TOUR OF THE FEDERAL BUILDINGS

Many of our country's most important buildings are located in Washington, D.C. Capitol Hill is the site of two majestic buildings that symbolize the spirit of America—the Supreme Court and the Capitol.

The Capitol is home of the United States Senate and the House of Representatives, two governing bodies that make up the legislative branch of the United States government. The Senate chamber is located in the north wing of the building, and the House of Representatives meets in the south wing. Senators and representatives meet in the Capitol to discuss the passing of new laws. When new presidents are elected, they are inaugurated into office inside the Capitol.

The Capitol is also a grandiose building. Thousands of tourists visit the Capitol to take a tour of some of its 540 rooms. Throughout history,

The Capitol is one of the most magnificent buildings in Washington, D.C.

many historic events took place in the Capitol. In the 1800s, politicians debated the issue of slavery in the Old Senate Chamber, and many past presidents signed bills into law in the President's Room. You can also see exhibits about past members of the Supreme Court in the Old Supreme Court Chamber, and statues of important historical figures from each state on display in National Statuary Hall.

Just a few steps away from the Capitol is the Supreme Court. Compared to other, very old, symbols of American democracy, the Supreme Court building is quite new. Built between 1932 and 1935, this building was completed 145 years after the Supreme Court first met in New York. From 1810 until 1860, the Court conducted business inside the Old Supreme Court Chamber within the Capitol.

The United States Supreme Court is the highest court in the nation. It is from this building that nine Supreme Court justices interpret our country's laws. Because of the Court's importance, the building is the site of many demonstrations, or gatherings, to protest laws that people feel are unfair.

As with the Capitol, the Supreme Court is also an impressive sight. Sixteen white marble columns stand outside the front entrance, and above the columns is written the famous phrase "Equal Justice Under Law." Signifying the importance of what goes on inside, the bronze entrance doors are oversized and weigh approximately 13 tons! Inside,

The Supreme Court building is an important symbol of our country's government.

court sessions take place in the Court Chamber. There are 24 marble columns in the Chamber and a raised Bench on which the justices sit. Visitors are invited to watch the Court in session.

The home of the president, called the White House, is located down the street from the Capitol building, at 1600 Pennsylvania Avenue. The White House is not only the First Family's home, it is also a symbol of the executive branch of the United States government. Before President Theodore Roosevelt decided to call it "The White House" in 1901, it went by such names as "The President's House," "The President's Palace," and "The Executive Mansion."

The name "White House" came about because the building had a white sandstone exterior, making it stand out from the red brick buildings in town.

As the personal home and office of the president, the White House is the site of many historic events. It is the place where presidents meet with leaders of foreign countries, and sign or veto bills that come through from Congress.

Every day more than 6,000 people visit the White House. Many rooms are open to the public, including the East Room, the scene of many historic White House events. The East Room was traditionally used for large gatherings, such as during the Civil War, when Union troops occupied the room for a period of time. A full-length portrait of George Washington hangs in the East Room. It is one of the few objects that has been in the White House since 1800. Other rooms include the State Dining Room, which is used for formal dinners and seats 140 guests. The China Room houses a collection of glassware and china that represents every president who has lived in the White House.

Although the Capitol, the Supreme Court, and the White House may be the city's most well-known buildings, there's much more to see and do in the capital city. In the next chapter you will find out more about the people and places of Washington.

The State Dining Room is one of the largest rooms in the White House.

51

CHAPTER FIVE

THE PEOPLE AND PLACES OF WASHINGTON, D.C.

Two thousand American elms line the National Mall.

As the capital of the United States, Washington, D.C. is an international city. People from all over the world have made the District their home. The city's many museums, parks, and architectural treasures make Washington, D.C. a great place to live and work. Colleges such as Georgetown University, Howard University, and George Washington University attract a large number of people to the city. Also, many people who live just outside the city consider themselves Washingtonians.

MEET THE PEOPLE

According to the 2000 census, Washington, D.C. is home to 572,059 people. The majority of the population—six of every ten people—is African-American. Three of every ten people are of European descent.

People of Hispanic origin make up almost eight of every hundred Washingtonians, and almost three of every hundred residents are Asian or Pacific Islanders. The remaining portion of the District's population is made up of other ethnicities, including American Indian.

Since so many residents are African-American, it is only natural that they have long played a large role in the city's government. Some well-known African-Americans in Washington politics today are Congresswoman Eleanor Holmes Norton, and Mayor Anthony Williams, as well as several members of the city council.

WHO'S WHO IN WASHINGTON, D.C.?

Eleanor Holmes Norton (1937–) has served five terms as the District of Columbia's elected, non-voting Congresswoman since 1991. She is a strong supporter of the city's fight for statehood.

People of all backgrounds live and work in Washington, D.C.

This photo shows a street in Anacostia, a neighborhood in southeast Washington, D.C.

Although the average income of D.C. residents is high by United States standards, the percentage of the city's population that lives in poverty is the highest in the nation. Like other major cities, Washington also has problems with its crime rate, an issue that receives much publicity because the crimes occur in our nation's capital. The people of Washington, D.C. are aware of these problems and are working hard to solve them. The city currently has many programs to improve the area's schools and to help unemployed residents find work.

WORKING IN WASHINGTON, D.C.

Some states are associated with particular industries, such as Michigan with the auto industry, and Texas with oil wells. Washington, D.C. is associated with government and tourism. These two industries mean the world to Washington. Almost everyone who lives in the city works in either government or tourism.

Tourism is big business in Washington. Tourism is the business of providing food, shelter, and entertainment to the city's more than 20 million visitors every year. Junior high school students, politicians, diplomats, sightseers, art lovers, and many others come to see the government in action, or to visit the city's many museums, monuments, and historic sites. Tourist-related industries, such as hotels, restaurants, and car-rental companies, employ about 50,000 people in Washington, D.C.

If there's one thing in Washington that's more common than tourists, it's the government. The government is the city's main employer, providing jobs for about 185,000 people. The city's many government buildings are filled with people who make their living as civil servants.

Hundreds of Washington, D.C. workers commute from their homes outside the city by car or by Metrorail.

But not everyone who works in the government lives in Washington, D.C. Some people live in hotels for a few months and return to their home states after their government business is finished. Many others—about 120,000—live in the nearby suburbs of Maryland and Virginia and commute to Washington for work. The Washington, D.C. metropolitan area includes surrounding areas such as Gaithersburg, Maryland, and Ashburn and Springfield in Virginia. If you count all the people who live in and around our nation's capital, its population jumps from 523,124 to 4.5 million.

Government jobs are part of what is known as the service industry. Many Washingtonians work in other service industries such as healthcare, finance, accounting, or law, among other things. Other jobs include education, communications, and transportation.

(TAKING A TOUR OF WASHINGTON, D.C.)

Washington, D.C. lies in the center of a circular highway. Because it surrounds the city and resembles a belt, this highway is called the Capital Beltway. The Capitol building is at the center of the city, and the streets surrounding the Capitol serve as dividing lines for the city's four parts, called quadrants: Northeast, Northwest, Southeast, and Southwest. Each quadrant consists of individual neighborhoods, such as Georgetown, Dupont Circle, Anacostia, and Washington Heights.

A tour of Washington, D.C. is very different from a tour of the states. While most tours go from city to city, a Washington, D.C. tour travels between quadrants and neighborhoods. Let's start our tour in the largest quadrant, the Northwest.

Streets in the capital city follow the original plan developed by L'Enfant in the late 1700s.

Cornbread is popular throughout the United States, but it holds a special meaning for Washington, D.C. After all, where would the city be without the corn that helped Washington's earliest settlers to survive?

CORNBREAD

(makes 8–9 servings)
1 cup all-purpose flour
1 cup cornmeal
2–4 tablespoons sugar
1 tablespoon baking powder
1/2 teaspoon salt
2 eggs
1 cup milk
1/4 cup cooking oil

1. Grease bottom and a small part of sides of a 9x9 baking pan.
2. Combine flour, cornmeal, sugar, baking powder, and salt in a mixing bowl. Make a well in center of mixture.
3. In another bowl, beat eggs.
4. Add milk and cooking oil to eggs.
5. Pour egg mixture into the bowl with the dry mixture. Stir until moist.
6. Pour batter into greased pan.
7. Bake at 425° for 20–25 minutes.

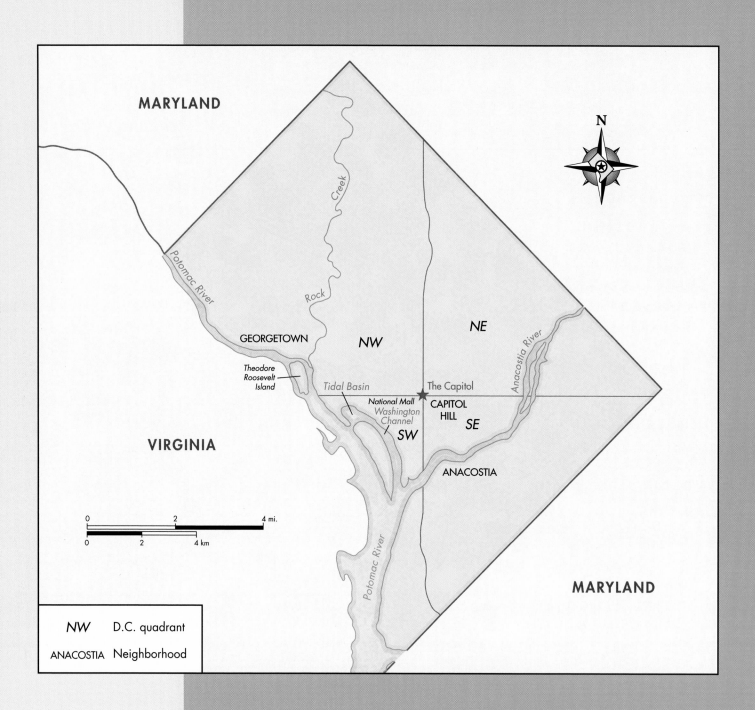

MARYLAND

Potomac River

Creek

Rock

GEORGETOWN

Theodore
Roosevelt
Island

VIRGINIA

Tidal Basin

National Mall
Washington
Channel

NW

The Capitol

CAPITOL
HILL

SW

SE

NE

Anacostia River

ANACOSTIA

Potomac River

MARYLAND

N

0   2   4 mi.

0   2   4 km

NW	D.C. quadrant
ANACOSTIA	Neighborhood

The Northwest quadrant covers the largest area in Washington, D.C. Development in this area began in the 1870s, mostly east of Rock Creek. Some of the neighborhoods in this part of the city include Shaw, Brightwood Park, the Palisades, Cathedral Heights, Crestwood, Fox Hall Village, and many others.

Most of Washington's well-known sights are in the Northwest quadrant. Within the quadrant there are several areas of distinction, including the National Mall and Capitol Hill.

Downtown

The downtown area of Washington, D.C., located near the National Mall, includes several of the city's most popular tourist destinations. It is a small section that takes up only 15 city blocks.

One of the most popular places in D.C.'s downtown is the White House, which receives more than 6,000 visitors each day. Another top attraction is the FBI tour. This one-hour tour takes visitors through the FBI laboratory to show how case evidence is examined. Tour guides discuss how the FBI works and tell stories about famous cases. There is also an exhibit on the "Ten Most Wanted Fugitives," with posters, newspaper clippings, and photographs of the list's history.

Other places of interest include Ford's Theatre, where Abraham Lincoln was assassinated in 1865. Plays and musicals are still performed at the theater, which was declared a National Historic Site in 1970. Across

WHO'S WHO IN WASHINGTON, D.C.?

J. Edgar Hoover (1895–1972) served as Director of the FBI from 1924 to 1972. During his leadership of almost 50 years, Hoover became a central figure in United States politics, and the FBI grew in efficiency and importance. Hoover was born in Washington, D.C.

the street from Ford's Theatre is the Petersen House, where Lincoln died. The house has been preserved to look just as it did on the historic night of April 14, 1865.

The National Aquarium is also located in downtown Washington, D.C. The Aquarium houses alligators, sharks, and piranhas. It also hosts special events such as Shark Day, when visitors can see six species of sharks—including baby sharks—and watch them being fed.

National Mall

The National Mall is the single most-popular tourist attraction in the city of Washington. Located on the dividing line between the Northwest and Southwest quadrants, the National Mall is the site of the Washington Monument, the Lincoln Memorial, the Vietnam Veterans' Memorial, the Smithsonian museums, and the National Gallery of Art. And that's just for starters. Let's take a closer look at some of the Mall's highlights.

Several of the museums along the Mall are part of the Smithsonian Institution, a research center and collector of artifacts. The National Air

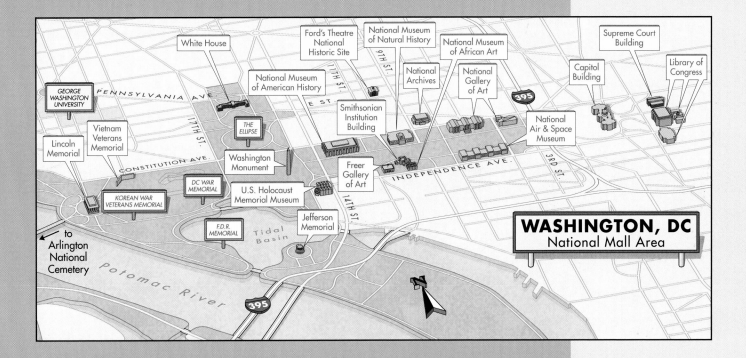

White House

Ford's Theatre National Historic Site

National Museum of Natural History

National Museum of African Art

Supreme Court Building

Library of Congress

GEORGE WASHINGTON UNIVERSITY

National Museum of American History

National Archives

National Gallery of Art

Capitol Building

PENNSYLVANIA AVE.

E ST.

9TH ST.

11TH ST.

395

Vietnam Veterans Memorial

THE ELLIPSE

Smithsonian Institution Building

Lincoln Memorial

17TH ST.

Washington Monument

National Air & Space Museum

CONSTITUTION AVE.

DC WAR MEMORIAL

U.S. Holocaust Memorial Museum

Freer Gallery of Art

INDEPENDENCE AVE.

3RD ST.

KOREAN WAR VETERANS MEMORIAL

14TH ST.

F.D.R. MEMORIAL

Tidal Basin

Jefferson Memorial

to Arlington National Cemetery

Potomac River

395

WASHINGTON, DC
National Mall Area

61

Inside the National Air and Space Museum is an amazing collection of air and spacecraft, most of which were flown at some point in history.

and Space Museum is part of the Smithsonian. It houses exhibits relating to the history, science, and technology of aviation and space flight. From early hang gliders to modern rockets, the museum contains the world's largest collection of historic aircraft and spacecraft. Displays include the *Fokker T-2*, the first aircraft to fly nonstop coast-to-coast in 1923, and the Wright brothers' first aircraft.

Another Smithsonian museum is the National Museum of Natural History. The museum is dedicated to understanding the natural world and our place in it. The dinosaur exhibit has real fossils from dinosaurs that lived between 213 and 144 million years ago. It also shows a scene from 70 million years ago, just before dinosaurs disappeared from Earth forever. If you prefer smaller creatures, don't miss the Insect Zoo. Spiders and other insects crawl around the zoo, where you can learn more about them and how they have survived over millions of years. Another interesting exhibit is the Hall of Bones, where skeletons of humans, gorillas, fish, and other animals are on display.

Aside from museums, the Mall is home to many of our nation's most important monuments. The Lincoln Memorial, located at the west end of the Mall, was built to look like a Greek temple. Thirty-six columns (representing the 36 states in the Union at the time of Lincoln's presidency) surround a sculpture of Lincoln seated inside the memorial chamber. The monument stands as a tribute to our country's 16th president and the nation he fought to save during the Civil War. Not far from the Lincoln Memorial is the Jefferson Memorial, which was built in honor of our third president, Thomas Jefferson. Inside this domed marble structure stands a 19-foot (6-m) statue of Jefferson on a pedestal. Although the memorial was dedicated in 1943, the bronze statue of Jefferson did not arrive there until four years later!

Georgetown

Northwest of the downtown area is Georgetown. As Washington's oldest neighborhood, Georgetown was originally founded in 1751 as an independent town. Although it became part of Washington, D.C. in 1878,

Quotations taken directly from Thomas Jefferson's writings are etched into the walls of the Jefferson Memorial.

Georgetown continued to govern itself as a separate city until 1895. The Georgetown neighborhood has always been a popular place to live and visit. Georgetown University is located in this area. Another well-known university, George Washington University, is in a neighborhood not far from Georgetown called Foggy Bottom.

There are several historic attractions in Georgetown. A Colonial house museum known as Old Stone House is believed to be the oldest building in the District of Columbia. Built in 1765, the house has been preserved to show what life was like in colonial days. You can also learn about the city's past by visiting Tudor Place Historic House and Garden, a mansion from the early 1800s. Finally, you can get a nice view of Georgetown by taking a barge ride along the Chesapeake and Ohio Canal, which runs from Georgetown to Cumberland, Maryland.

Capitol Hill

Capitol Hill is located in the southeast part of the Northwest quadrant. This area is home to the Capitol, Washington's tallest building. The Capitol building isn't all you'll find here. The Supreme Court, the Library of Congress, the United States Botanic Garden, the National Postal Museum, and Union Station are also on the Hill. Located next to these public buildings are private residences. This area, known for its beauty and safety, attracts many D.C. residents.

This photo shows a residential neighborhood in Capitol Hill.

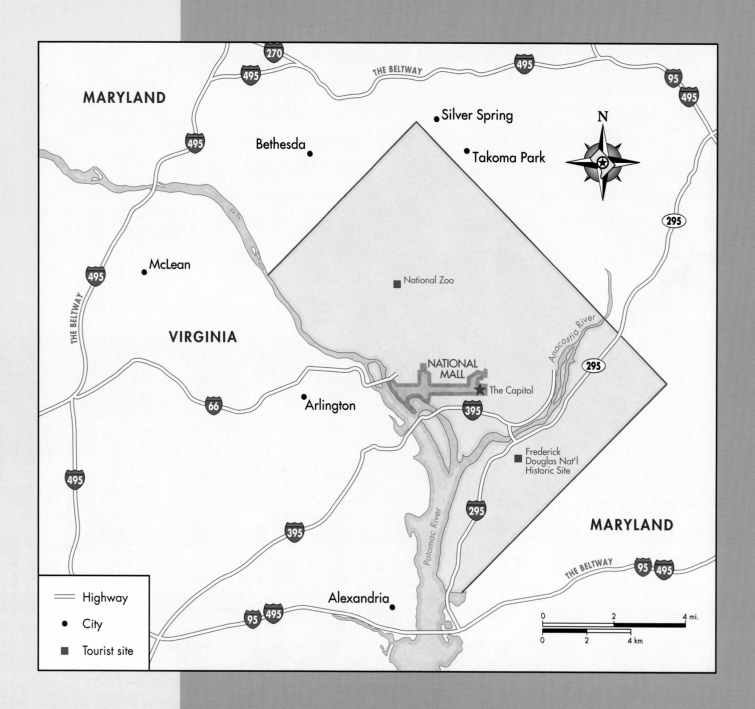

MARYLAND

270

495

THE BELTWAY

495

95
495

Silver Spring

Bethesda

Takoma Park

N

495

McLean

295

VIRGINIA

■ National Zoo

Anacostia River

NATIONAL
MALL

295

★ The Capitol

66

Arlington

395

295

Frederick
Douglas Nat'l
Historic Site

MARYLAND

495

THE BELTWAY

95
495

Potomac River

Alexandria

95
495

Highway

City

Tourist site

0   2   4 mi.

0   2   4 km

NORTHEAST QUADRANT

Northeast Washington, D.C. is a mostly residential part of the city. In recent years, new neighborhoods have been created in this area and technology companies have located here. Several universities are also in the Northeast quadrant, including Howard University, Gallaudet University, and the Catholic University of America.

The National Arboretum is a showcase for trees, shrubs, flowers, and other plants. Every year, more than 500,000 people visit this 446-acre (180-ha) display. At the Arboretum's Washington Youth Garden, students try their hand at gardening. They learn about plant studies through the Arboretum, and then put their knowledge to work in a real life garden on site.

SOUTHWEST QUADRANT

The Southwest quadrant is the smallest area in Washington, D.C. In the 1950s and 1960s, this area went through a period of renewal, in which many existing buildings were torn down and new housing developments were built. Today, it is a mix of high-rise apartment buildings, townhouses, and green areas. It is a busy waterfront community full of restaurants, river views, and lots of boating activity.

Some of the area's old structures still stand, such as Wheat Row, the first row houses built in the city. Another building that survived the demolition is St. Dominic's Church, built in 1875. The church's 250-foot (76-m) spire is an awesome sight.

A large portion of Anacostia's residents are African-American.

Southeast Washington is mostly residential, with many row houses, single family homes, and apartments. The north and west parts of this area are filled with federal and office buildings.

Anacostia, a neighborhood on the southeast bank of the Anacostia River, was the first suburb of Washington, D.C. It was built mainly for workers of the nearby Navy Yard, a site that George Washington chose in 1799 to protect the area from enemy ships sailing up the Potomac River. The historic district of Anacostia has more than 500 buildings dating from about 1854 to 1930. Although some are in disrepair, many stand in proud remembrance of the neighborhood's rich African-American history, including churches and schools. The Navy Yard is home to a Navy Museum that features exhibits about Navy battles and wartime heroes.

Other interesting sites in this area include the Frederick Douglass National Historic Site, former home of the famous and influ-

WHO'S WHO IN WASHINGTON, D.C.?

Frederick Douglass (1817–1895) was one of our country's greatest leaders of the abolitionist movement, which fought to end slavery in the United States. Born a slave in Maryland, he escaped in 1838. He began speaking on behalf of the American Anti-Slavery Society and eventually became recognized as one of America's first great African-American speakers. He served as an advisor to President Lincoln during the Civil War and is remembered for his contributions on behalf of human rights. He lived in Washington, D.C.

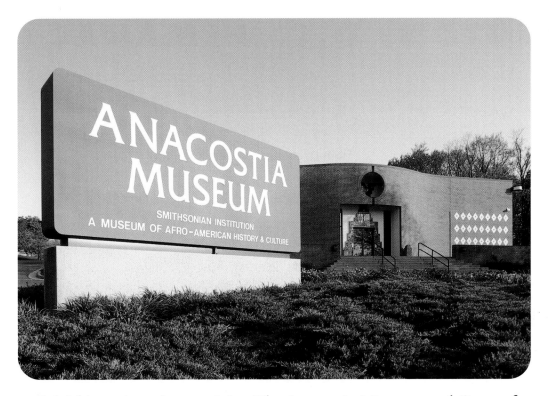

The Anacostia Museum focuses on African-American history and culture around Washington, Maryland, Virginia, Georgia, and the Carolinas.

ential African-American activist. The Anacostia Museum and Center for African-American History and Culture is also located in Anacostia. The museum contains many exhibits about African-American experiences through history.

WASHINGTON, D.C. ALMANAC

Founding date: Became the nation's capital in 1800

District seal: The seal shows the figure of a woman representing Justice putting a wreath on George Washington's statue. The Potomac River is in the background. Adopted in 1871.

District flag: The flag has three red stars above two red stripes on a white field. The design is based on George Washington's coat of arms. Adopted in 1938.

Geographic center: Near Fourth and L Streets Northwest

Total area/rank: 68 square miles (177 sq km)/51st

Borders: Maryland and Virginia

Latitude and longitude: Washington, D.C. is located approximately between 38° 50' and 39° 00' N and 76° 50' and 77°10' W

Highest/lowest elevation: Tenleytown at the Reno Reservoir, 410 feet (125 m) above sea level/sea level

Hottest/coldest temperature: 106°F (41°C) on July 20, 1930/–15°F (–26°C) on February 11, 1899

Land area/rank: 61 square miles (158 sq km)/51st

Inland water area/rank: 7 square miles (18 sq km)/51st

Population (2000 census): 572,059

Origin of district name: Christopher Columbus and George Washington

Wards: 8

District government: 13 city council members

Major rivers: Potomac River, Anacostia River

Bird: Wood Thrush

Flower: American Beauty Rose

Motto: *Justitia Omnibus,* Justice for All

Nickname: Nation's Capital

Song: "The Star-Spangled Banner" by Francis Scott Key (1814)

Tree: Scarlet Oak

TIMELINE

WASHINGTON, D.C. HISTORY

Captain John Smith sails the Potomac to Washington

Congress and the president move to Washington

Congress abolishes slavery in Washington, D.C.

Leonard Calvert arrives to settle Maryland

Jacob Funk builds the area's first factories

Washington area is chosen as the U.S. capital

Abraham Lincoln is assassinated at Ford's Theatre

Georgetown is founded

British invade and set fire to Washington

Congress returns Alexandria to Virginia

| 1608 | 1634 | 1752 | 1765 | 1790 | 1800 | 1814 | 1846 | 1851 | 1865 |

| 1607 | 1620 | | 1776 | 1783 | 1787 | 1812–15 | 1843 | 1846–48 | 1861–65 |

The first permanent British settlement at Jamestown, Virginia

American Revolutionary War ends

Pioneers travel west on the Oregon Trail

Pilgrims set up Plymouth colony

U.S. Constitution is written

U.S. fights war with Mexico

American colonies declare independence from England

U.S. and England fight the War of 1812

Civil War occurs in the United States

UNITED STATES HISTORY

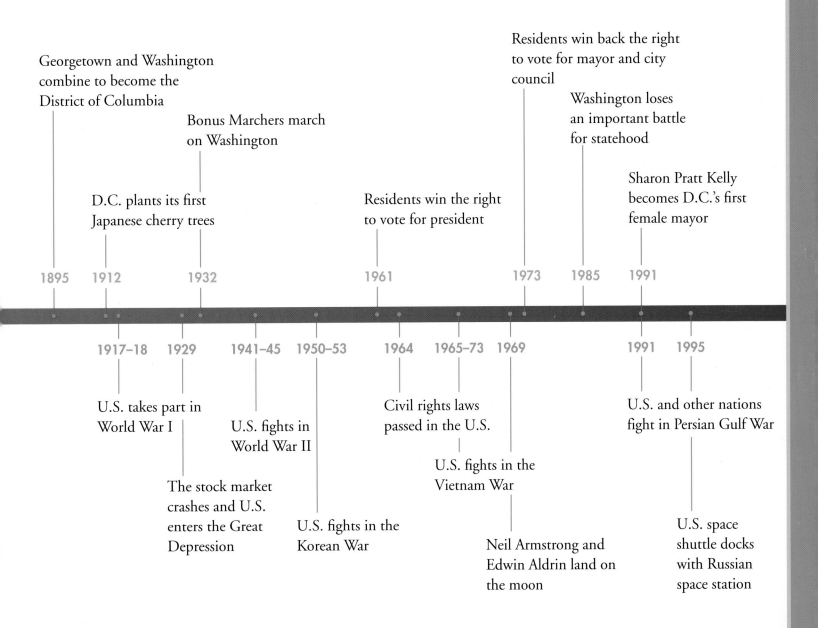

Georgetown and Washington combine to become the District of Columbia

Bonus Marchers march on Washington

D.C. plants its first Japanese cherry trees

Residents win back the right to vote for mayor and city council

Washington loses an important battle for statehood

Residents win the right to vote for president

Sharon Pratt Kelly becomes D.C.'s first female mayor

1895   1912   1932   1961   1973   1985   1991

1917–18   1929   1941–45   1950–53   1964   1965–73   1969   1991   1995

U.S. takes part in World War I

U.S. fights in World War II

Civil rights laws passed in the U.S.

U.S. and other nations fight in Persian Gulf War

The stock market crashes and U.S. enters the Great Depression

U.S. fights in the Vietnam War

U.S. fights in the Korean War

Neil Armstrong and Edwin Aldrin land on the moon

U.S. space shuttle docks with Russian space station

GALLERY OF FAMOUS WASHINGTONIANS

Edward Albee
(1928–)
One of America's leading playwrights. Winner of three Pulitzer Prizes and two Tony Awards. Born in Washington, D.C.

Connie Chung
(1946–)
Well-known television journalist. Born in Washington, D.C.

John Foster Dulles
(1888–1959)
A lawyer and diplomat. He served as secretary of state under President Dwight D. Eisenhower from 1953 to 1959. Dulles Airport is named after him. Born in Washington, D.C.

Marvin Gaye
(1939–1984)
A popular singer, and the best-selling Motown artist of all time. Born in Washington, D.C.

Katherine Graham
(1917–2001)
Publisher of *The Washington Post* and CEO of The Washington Post Company. She won a Pulitzer Prize for her autobiography, *Personal History*. Lived in Washington, D.C.

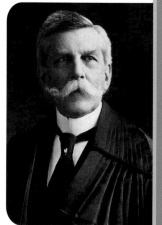

Oliver Wendell Holmes Jr.
(1841–1935)
Served as a United States Supreme Court justice for thirty years. Born in Massachusetts and died in Washington, D.C.

John F. Kennedy, Jr.
(1960–1999)
Well-loved son of President John F. Kennedy and Jacqueline Kennedy. Publisher of *George* magazine. He was mourned by millions when he died in a plane crash off the coast of Massachusetts. Born in Washington, D.C.

Pete Sampras
(1971–)
Tennis great with a total of 12 Grand Slam Championship wins to his name. He was the top tennis player in the world from 1993 to 1998. Born in Washington, D.C.

John Philip Sousa
(1854–1932)
American bandmaster and composer of more than 100 marches. Born in Washington, D.C.

GLOSSARY

assassinate: to kill someone, usually for political or religious reasons

charter: an official document granting rights to a new borough, company, or other organization

civil servants: people who work in public-service or government jobs, such as public school teachers, policemen, public librarians, firemen, and politicians

colonization: the process of sending citizens to new territories to form stronger ties to the new land

colony: a new territory peopled by a group from a more established country

demolition: the destruction of a building or other structure

manorial system: a system in which tenants pay a fixed rent to the proprietor or landlord

natural boundary: geographical features such as rivers, lakes, or mountain ranges that divide one area from another

persecute: to cause suffering, to harass

plantation: huge farms in the South that were worked by slave labor

political representation: the process of acting on the behalf of other people within the field of politics

sacred ground: holy land

statehood: the position of being a state in the United States

sturgeon: a kind of fish that was once plentiful in the Anacostia River

tidal basin: an artificial body of water open to a river or stream and subject to tidal action

urban: having the characteristics of a city

veteran: a person who has served as a soldier

veto: the right of the governor to override a decision of the legislature

FOR MORE INFORMATION

Web sites

District of Columbia: Homepage

http://www.washingtondc.gov/

Provides information about the city government, including the mayor's office and the city council.

The National Park Service, Washington, D.C.

http://www.cr.nps.gov/nr/travel/wash/dcmap.htm

This site offers information about Washington's historic neighborhoods, buildings, and monuments.

Official Washington, D.C. Homepage

http://www.dchomepage.net/

Everything you ever wanted to know about visiting D.C., including where to stay, what to see, what to do, and how to get around.

White House for Kids

http://www.whitehouse.gov/kids/index.html

President Bush's website for young Americans. Includes photos of the White House and information about the president and First Lady, as well as the vice president.

Books

Ashabranner, Brent. *No Better Hope: What the Lincoln Memorial Means to America.* Twenty First Century Books, 2001.

Harness, Cheryl. *George Washington.* Washington, D.C.: National Geographic Society, 2000.

Russell, Sharman Apt. *Frederick Douglass.* Broomall, PA: Chelsea House, 1989.

Silberdick Feinberg, Barbara. *The Changing White House.* Danbury, CT: Children's Press, 2000.

Addresses

Government of the District of Columbia

John A. Wilson Building
1350 Pennsylvania Avenue NW
Washington, D.C. 20004

Washington, D.C. Convention and Tourism Corporation

1212 New York Avenue NW, Suite 600
Washington, D.C. 20005

INDEX

Page numbers in *italics* indicate illustrations

Adams, John, 23, 27
agriculture, 18
All the President's Men, 39
American Revolution, 22
Anacostia, *54,* 68
Anacostia Museum, 69, *69*
Anacostia River, 12

Baltimore, Lord, 16
Banneker, Benjamin, 26, *26*
basketball, 63
Beall, George, 20
Beltway. *See* Capital Beltway
Bengough, W., 32
Bernstein, Carl, 39
Bonus March, 35, *35*
Booth, John Wilkes, 31, *31*

Calvert, George, 16
Calvert, Leonard, 16, 17–18
capital
    aerial view, *56*
    agreement on location, 23–24
    construction, 24–27, 28, 32
    early years, 27–29
    expansion, 33
Capital Beltway, 56
Capitol building, *13, 46, 47,* 48
Capitol Hill, 65, *65*
cherry trees, 9, *9,* 10
Chung, Connie, 74
civil rights, 36–37
Civil War, 29–31
climate, 12–14
colonies, English, 21–22
commuters, 55, *55*
Confederate States of America, 29
Congress, 23, 32–33, 43, 44, 46
cornbread (recipe), 57
crime, 54

Declaration of Independence, 21, *22*
Depression. *See* Great Depression
Douglass, Frederick, 68
Dulles, John Foster, 74

Easter Egg Roll, 51
Eastern Seaboard, 7
Eighth Regiment Massachusetts Volunteer
        Militia, 30, *30*
Eisenhower, Dwight, 36
Ellicott, Andrew, 26, *26*
Ellington, Duke, 60, *60*
Emancipation Proclamation, 30
employment, 54–56
English colonies, 21–22

Farmer's Almanac, 26
farming, 18
FBI, 59
federal buildings, 46–51
Federal City, 24
festivals, 10
Fleete, Henry, 16
Foggy Bottom, 21
football, 63, *63*
Ford's Theatre, 31, *31,* 59–60
forests, 8
Funk, Jacob, 20–21
Funkstown, 20–21

Gaye, Marvin, 74
geography, 4, 7
    landscape, 8–9
    map, *11*
    quadrants, 56, *58,* 59–69
    rivers and streams, 8, 9–12
Georgetown, 20, 33, 63–65
Georgetown Rowing Crew, *7*
Georgetown University, *64*
Gordon, George, 20
government, 45
    city history, 43–44, 46
    Congress, 23, 32–33, 43, 44, 46

Constitution, 23
Declaration of Independence, 21, *22*
employment, 55–56
executive branch, 41–42
Home Rule Act, 46
judicial branch, 43
legislative branch, 42
New Deal, 36
statehood, 46
Graham, Katherine, *74, 74*
Great Depression, 34–36
Great Falls, 10, *10*

Hall of Bones, 62
hockey, 63
Hoffman, Dustin, *39*
Holmes, Oliver Wendell, Jr., *74, 74*
Hoover, Herbert, 35
Hoover, J. Edgar, 59, *59*
housing, 32, 36

independence, 21–22
Insect Zoo, 62

Japan, 10
Jefferson, Thomas, 27, 64
Jefferson Building, *34*
Jefferson Memorial, 63, *63*

Kennedy, John F., 36
Kennedy, John F., Jr., 74
King, Martin Luther, Jr., 36–37, *37*

landscape, 8–9
legislators inside the Capitol, *44*
L'Enfant, Pierre Charles, 24–26, *25*
Library of Congress, *34*
Lincoln, Abraham, 29, *29*, 31, *31*
Lincoln Memorial, *4*, 63

maps
    animated attractions, *6*
    geographical, *11*
    major highways, *66*
    National Mall, *61*
    quadrants, *58*

March on Washington, 36–37
mayor, 41–42, 43
McMillan model, 33
monuments, 63
museums, *61, 62, 65, 68–69*

Nacotchtank Indians, 15
National Air and Space Museum, 62, *62*
National Aquarium, 60
National Arboretum, 67
National Cherry Blossom Festival, 10
National Mall, *52, 59*, 60, *61, 62–63*
National Museum of Natural History,
        62
National Statuary Hall, 48
Native Americans, 16–17
    and European diseases, 18
    Nacotchtank, 15
    Piscataway, 15, 16–18
    Susquehannock, 18
Navy Yard, 68
New Deal, 36
Nixon, Richard M., 38, *39*
Northeast quadrant, 67
Northwest quadrant, 59
    Capitol Hill, 65, *65*
    downtown, 59–60
    Georgetown, 63–65
    National Mall, 60, *61, 62–63*
Norton, Eleanor Holmes, 53

Old Congressional Library, *32*
Old Stone House, 65

Pentagon, 39, 40, *40*
people
    African-American, 32, 36–37
    European, 16–22
    Native American, 15, 16–18
    population diversity, 52–53
    slavery, 18–19, *19*, 29
Petersen House, 60
Piscataway Indians, 15, 16–18
plantations, 18–19
plant life, 8, 9
pollution, 12

population, 31, 32, 33, 34, 52–53, 55
Potomac River, *7, 9–10, 10, 17*
poverty, *54*
presidential address, *44*
presidential reception, *27*

quadrants, 56, *58*
    Northeast, 67
    Northwest, 59–65
    Southeast, 68–69
    Southwest, 67

Redford, Robert, *39*
Redskins. *See* Washington Redskins
Revolutionary War, 22
rivers and streams, 8, 9–12
Rock Creek Park, 8, *8*
Roosevelt, Franklin D., 36, *36*
Roosevelt, Theodore, 50

Sampras, Pete, 74, *74*
Second Continental Congress, *22*
service industry, 56
shipping and trade, 20
slavery, 18–19, *19, 29*
Smith, John, 16
Smithsonian Institution, 60
Sousa, John Philip, 74
Southeast quadrant, 68–69
Southwest quadrant, 67
Spofford, Ainsworth Rand, *32*
sports, 63
St. Dominic's Church, 67
State Dining Room, *51*
statehood, 46

Supreme Court building, 48, *49, 50*
Susquehannock Indians, 18

taxation, 21
terrorism, 39
Tidal Basin, 9, *9*
timeline, historic, 72–73
time zones, 8
tobacco, 18–19, 20
tourism, 9, 54–55
trade and shipping, 20
transportation
    Capital Beltway, 56, *66*
    Metrorail, *55*
    roadways/highways, 28, 36, *55*
Tudor Place Historic House and Garden,
    65

War for Independence, 22
War of 1812, 28, *28*
Washington, George, 23, *23,* 24–25,
    25, 26, 27, 43
Washington Monument, *9*
Washington Redskins, *63*
Washington Youth Garden, 67
waterfalls, 10, *10*
Watergate, *38,* 38–39
water pollution, 12
Wheat Row, 67
Whispering Gallery, 48
White House, *41, 50,* 50–51, 59
Williams, Anthony, 42, *42,* 53
Woodward, Bob, 39
World Trade Center, 39
World War I, 33–34

ABOUT THE AUTHOR

Elina Furman has written more than 20 books on a variety of subjects. She often writes with her sister, Leah Furman. She researched this book by reading about Washington, D.C., researching the Internet, and looking over photos of her trip to the District. What she remembers most about her time in Washington, D.C. are the *cicadas*, also known as locusts. They were the biggest bugs she'd ever seen and they were everywhere. Fortunately for Washingtonians, cicadas only come around once every seventeen years.